Spotlight on the
MAYA, AZTEC, and INCA CIVILIZATIONS

Ancient MAYA TECHNOLOGY

Charles C. Hofer

PowerKiDS press™

NEW YORK

Published in 2017 by The Rosen Publishing Group, Inc.
29 East 21st Street, New York, NY 10010

Editor: Caitlin McAneney
Book Design: Mickey Harmon

Photo Credits: Cover ventdusud/Shutterstock.com; p.5 Simon Dannhauer/Shutterstock.com; p. 6 Maks Narodenko/Shutterstock.com; p. 7 Viktor Kaposi/Moment/Getty Images; p. 9 (earflares) https://upload. wikimedia.org/wikipedia/commons/8/84/Flower-Shaped_Earflares_LACMA_M.2007.85.1-.2.jpg; p. 9 (jade ornament) Purchase, Jan and Marica Vilcek Gift, 2007/The Metropolitan Museum of Art; p. 11 Fer Gregory/ Shutterstock.com; p. 12 Kiev.Victor/Shutterstock.com; p. 13 Anatoli Styf/Shutterstock.com; p. 14 Jose Ignacio Soto/Shutterstock.com; p. 15 Brandt Bolding/Shutterstock.com; p. 16 Universal History Archive/Contributor/ Getty Images; p. 17 Arie v.d. Wolde/Shutterstock.com; p. 18 Terry W. Rutledge/Contributor/National Geographic/ Getty Images; p. 19 The Michael C. Rockefeller Memorial Collection, Gift of Nelson A. Rockefeller, 1963/The Metropolitan Museum of Art; p. 20 De Agostini/Archivio J. Lange/De Agostini Picture Library/Getty Images; p. 23 Jannis Tobias Werner/Shutterstock.com; p. 25 Rigamondis/Shutterstock.com; p. 26 https://en.wikipedia. org/wiki/Dresden_Codex#/media/File:Dresden_codex,_page_2.jpg; p. 27 https://upload.wikimedia.org/ wikipedia/commons/0/0f/Takalik_Abaj_Stela_5.JPG; p. 29 (inset) https://upload.wikimedia.org/wikipedia/ commons/8/8e/Grabado_de_Hern%C3%A1n_Cort%C3%A9s.jpg; p. 29 (main) https://upload.wikimedia.org/ wikipedia/commons/b/b4/Relief_Showing_Conquistador_Stamping_on_Mayan_Heads_-_Facade_of_Casa_de_ Montejo_-_16th_Century_Mansion_-_Merida_-_Mexico.jpg.

Library of Congress Cataloging-in-Publication Data

Names: Hofer, Charles author.
Title: Ancient Maya technology / Charles C. Hofer.
Description: New York : PowerKids Press, 2016. | Series: Spotlight on the
  Maya, Aztec, and Inca civilizations | Includes index.
Identifiers: LCCN 2016002139 | ISBN 9781508149040 (pbk.) | ISBN 9781499419832 (library bound) | ISBN 9781499419818 (6 pack)
Subjects: LCSH: Mayas--History--Juvenile literature. |
  Mayas--Antiquities--Juvenile literature. | Central
  America--Antiquities--Juvenile literature. | Mexico--Antiquities--Juvenile
  literature.
Classification: LCC F1435.3.I53 H65 2016 | DDC 972/.6--dc23
LC record available at http://lccn.loc.gov/2016002139

CPSIA Compliance Information: Batch #BS16PK: For further information contact Rosen Publishing, New York, New York at 1-800-237-9932.

CONTENTS

RISE OF THE MAYA

The lands of the ancient Maya stretch across parts of today's Mexico, Guatemala, Belize, El Salvador, and Honduras. Some areas are mountainous and covered in thick forests. Other lowland areas are swampy, with dense jungles along the coastline.

The Maya were great builders and are best known for their grand temples and palaces. They built **canals** to provide water to their people. They developed medicine and wrote books. They explored astronomy and invented advanced calendars based on their discoveries.

These advances in technology allowed the Maya culture to grow and prosper. Scattered populations of people grew into a strong civilization. Because of their advances, the Maya's small, simple villages eventually turned into great **city-states**. For hundreds of years, the Maya ruled over lands in today's Mexico and Central America, in what's known as Mesoamerica. This great culture and its advanced technology developed over thousands of years.

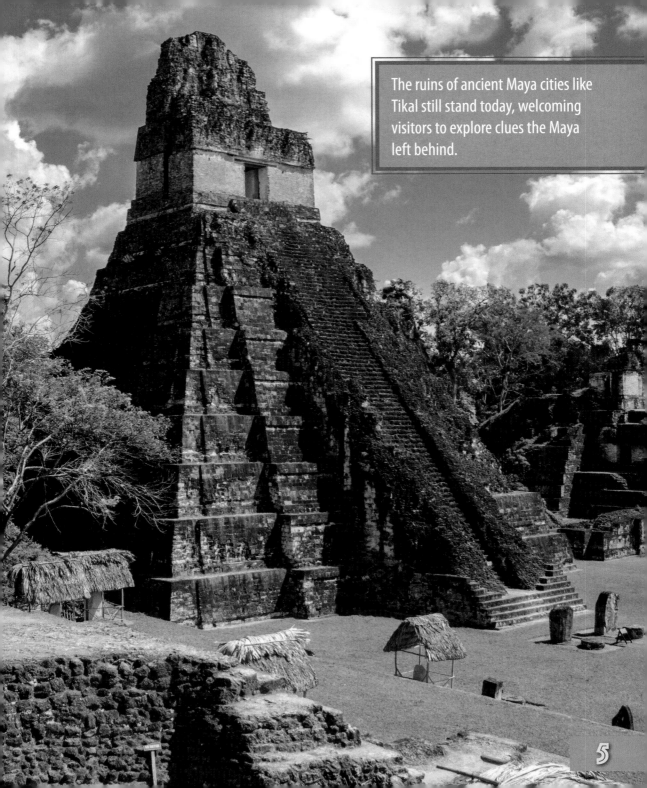

The ruins of ancient Maya cities like Tikal still stand today, welcoming visitors to explore clues the Maya left behind.

ADVANCES IN AGRICULTURE

The first people living in Maya lands were mostly hunter-gatherers, which means they hunted animals and gathered plants for food. However, by about 2000 BC, the Maya learned to grow maize, or corn. By growing maize and other crops, the Maya were able to settle small villages that led to a more permanent civilization.

The lowland coastal areas of the Maya region were difficult to farm due to large wetland areas and dense forests.

Maize was one of the most important ancient Maya crops. Today, Maya people still use maize in many of their meals.

This Maya canal is found in the ancient city of Palenque. Canals brought water to farmland and cities.

To manage the forest areas, the Maya used a slash-and-burn method of farming. They cleared large areas of forest by burning it. After the fire, the ashy soil would be rich for planting crops. The Maya also created a series of canals. These could be used to drain wetlands for use as farmland. These **techniques** were developed during a time called the Pre-Classic Period, during which the foundation of the Maya civilization was built.

USING ROCKS AND MINERALS

The lands of the Maya did not contain **iron ore**. Therefore, they couldn't make metal tools, unlike some other early civilizations. Instead, the Maya worked with hard minerals and rocks. Rocks, such as flint, were shaped into axes and other tools that could help clear forests and build houses.

Granite tools could be used to grind maize and prepare other foods. Obsidian, a strong volcanic glass, was sharpened and used for knives, spearheads, and other weapons. Even without strong metal, the Maya built massive temples, palaces, and roads.

The Maya also used their tools to make art and jewelry. The Maya collected jade, a beautiful green mineral that could be carved using flint tools. The Maya highly valued this precious stone, and some of the finest **artifacts** they left behind are carved from jade. Many Maya rulers have been found buried with jade jewelry and other pieces of jade art.

The Maya created jewelry and other art from jade, which is a valuable stone found in the highlands of Mesoamerica.

EXPANDING TERRITORY

By AD 250, the Maya entered what would become known as the Classic Period. This period lasted until about AD 900 and marked some of the most successful advances of that time.

During the Classic Period, Maya territory expanded to cover large areas of Mesoamerica. The Maya civilization consisted of dozens of scattered city-states. Between city-states were mountains, forests, and wetlands. The Maya would have to find a way to connect their city-states.

Many Maya cities, such as El Mirador, hosted a network of roads known as *sacbeob*. These roads began at the center of the city and crisscrossed through the swampy lowland areas. This made travel and trade easier and allowed the city to grow.

Archaeologists also believe the Maya built the largest **suspension bridge** in the ancient world. The bridge was located near the city of Yaxchilán. The bridge offered important access to the city during rainy seasons.

Maya cities such as Palenque flourished during the Classic Period. These are the ruins of the Temple of the Sun in Palenque.

PLASTER AND RUBBER

The Maya had to rely on natural resources found in their own lands. Their use of plaster and rubber greatly added to Maya life. Plaster was made from **limestone**. The Maya crushed limestone into a powder, burned it, and then added water to make the glue-like material. The plaster was then used as a **mortar** to join bricks together to make strong walls. It was also used as a coating on temples and other buildings. The Maya then painted or decorated these walls,

The Grand Ball Court at Chichén Itzá stills stands today as the largest ball court in all of Mesoamerica.

This is the "milk" that comes from rubber trees. It's used to make rubber.

creating pieces of art that told stories of Maya culture.

The Maya also made rubber with a sap-like liquid from local rubber trees and other materials. The rubber was used for many products, but it was especially important in making balls for the Maya ball games. These games played an important role in Maya culture and were important to their religion. Many Maya cities had impressive ball courts where the game was played.

THE MIGHTY TEMPLES

Religion was a very important part of Maya life. The Maya built huge stone temples to honor their gods and kings. These structures were mostly built out of limestone and volcanic rock.

Part of what made Maya temples so unique—and sturdy—was their arch design. Creating massive structures

Many people visit the Temple of Kukulkan each year to take a trip back in time to the height of the Maya civilization.

The corbel arch was a key invention that helped support massive temples.

out of stone wasn't easy. The largest Maya temples rose more than 200 feet (61 m) into the air! To make doorways and roofs, the Maya designed a support system now called the corbel arch or Maya arch.

These temples hosted religious ceremonies and other important events in Maya culture. For that reason, temples were the center of life in magnificent Maya city-states like Tikal. Many of these temples still stand today! Places like the Temple of Kukulkan in Chichén Itzá, Mexico, still welcome visitors to explore the ancient world of the Maya.

MEDICINE OF THE MAYA

The Maya were a very religious people. To them, medicine was a combination of science and religion. The Maya used local resources for medicine, but they also relied on religious rituals to help those in need.

Maya technology led to many advances in medicine. The Maya stitched wounds using human hair and shaped obsidian to create sharp blades used for surgery. They made casts to heal broken bones and they treated their sick with medicines made from local plants. The Maya regularly ate food made from cacao beans,

This ancient Maya artifact is a figurine of a kneeling woman, who may be a priestess or healer.

Cacao was used to treat many illnesses, from fever to poor appetite. It was also thought to improve digestion. The Maya believed cacao was given to them by a god.

which we use today to make chocolate. The Maya believed consuming cacao was healthy.

The Maya also believed in a strong balance between the body and the soul. Because of this, Maya healing practices were usually performed by *ah-men*. They were religious leaders who were held in high regard in Maya culture. The *ah-men* not only provided medicines to the sick but also provided spiritual guidance to heal people.

WRITINGS OF THE MAYA

The Maya advanced their civilization even further when they developed a written language. Some writing may have been created as early as 300 BC. Pictures and shapes, or glyphs, represented words or sounds. We call this kind of written language hieroglyphics. The Maya used glyphs to record their stories. They painted pottery with these images. They also carved glyphs into stone temples.

The Olmec civilization, which came before the Maya, also used glyphs in their written

This artwork shows a Maya artisan carving glyphs into stone.

Because many glyphs were carved in stone, they still exist today. This is a piece of a relief carving that predicted a terrible, violent day in the future. Some modern-day people took this story seriously, and thought the world would end on a certain day in the Maya calendar.

communication. Although the Maya weren't the first people of Mesoamerica to write, their advances in communication helped some of their stories survive.

The Maya also wrote many books, called codices. These books were written on an early form of paper made from fig tree bark. These books contained Maya astronomical discoveries and information on their calendar system. All but a handful of these books have been lost. The Spanish destroyed many in the 1500s.

THE NUMBER SYSTEM

One of the greatest advances of the Maya civilization was their number system. Numbers allowed the Maya to develop a system of **commerce** where goods and services could be bought and sold. A strong system of commerce allowed city-states to grow and prosper. Most importantly, this number system allowed the Maya to create an advanced calendar system.

The Maya number system consisted of just a few

Having a number system made it possible for the Maya to trade with one another fairly. These are the ruins of the marketplace of Chichén Itzá.

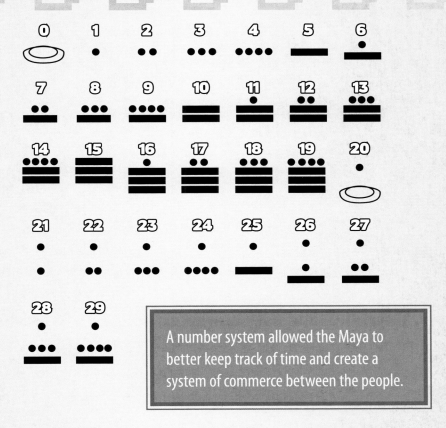

A number system allowed the Maya to better keep track of time and create a system of commerce between the people.

simple symbols. A dot represented one, a line represented five, and a shell-like shape represented zero. Combining these three symbols in different groups formed numbers. The Maya are often credited with being one of the first peoples to use the number zero.

The Maya based their number system on the number 20. Today, we base our number system on the number 10. Many believe the Maya used their number system because we have 20 fingers and toes.

LOOKING TO THE SKIES

The Maya took a great interest in astronomy. Many of their cultural beliefs were based on the sun, moon, stars, and planets. Several **observatories**, such as El Caracol in Chichén Itzá, still stand today.

Chichén Itzá is also home to the Temple of Kukulkan. This famous pyramid has exactly 365 steps, one for each day of the year. The temple was designed so that twice each year, during the spring and fall **equinoxes**, a shadow in the shape of a large snake falls across the temple. As the sun sets, the snake shadow slithers down the steps.

The Maya did not have advanced technology, such as telescopes, to study the skies. Scholars believe the Maya used simple tools, such as crossed sticks, to mark the changes to celestial, or space, bodies. Their work in astronomy allowed them to create one of their most important technological advances—the Maya calendars.

The important Maya city of Chichén Itzá is a great example of how important astronomy was to the Maya. The Temple of Kukulkan, or El Castillo, and the observatory El Caracol were built with astronomy in mind.

23

THE SACRED ROUND

The Maya calendars could be used for agriculture, following the movements of the stars and planets, and keeping track of yearly events. The Maya calendar system consisted of three separate calendars that played different roles in Maya life. The three calendars were represented as wheels with different symbols on them. The wheels turned together and different combinations of symbols represented different days.

The first part of the Maya calendar was the Sacred Round. Each day had special meaning and was connected to one of the many Maya gods. The Sacred Round was based on 260 days, which may have had to do with the approximate length of a human pregnancy. This calendar was composed of two wheels that turned with each other. The smaller wheel held 13 numbers while the larger wheel had 20 named days. The turning calendar helped the Maya determine religious ceremonies and other sacred dates throughout the year.

The two wheels on the left represent the Sacred Round, with its cycles of 13 and 20 days. The arc on the right represents the Maya's vague year of 365 days.

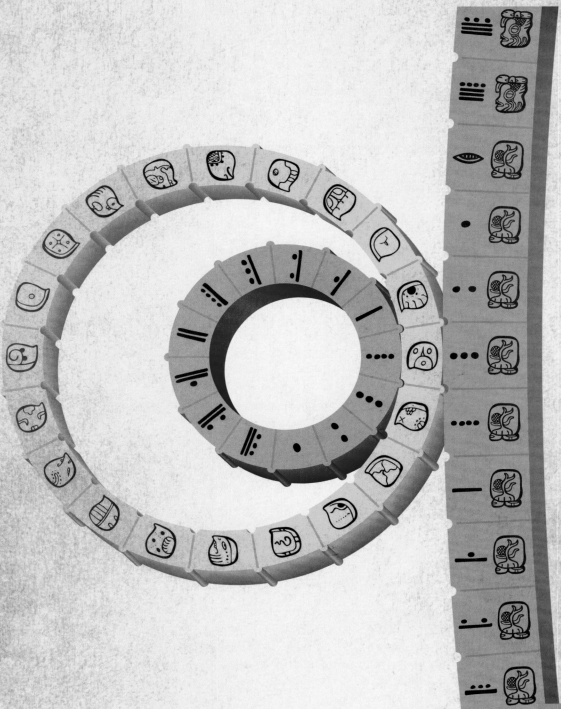

THE LONG COUNT

Along with the Sacred Round, the Maya calendar system also contained the vague year and the Long Count. The Maya vague year was divided into 18 months of 20 days each, for 360 days. Our modern calendar year is based on about 365 and one-quarter days. This is the time it takes Earth to orbit the sun. The extra one-quarter day is made up every four years when we add one more day to the month of February. The Maya, however, didn't account for this extra one-quarter of a day. The Maya added five extra days, called the uayeb, at the end of their year for a total of 365 days.

The third Maya calendar is the Long Count, which was used to record history. The Long Count started on August 11, 3114 BC, when, according to Maya legend, the world was created.

The Dresden Codex gave experts insight into how the Maya calendar system worked.

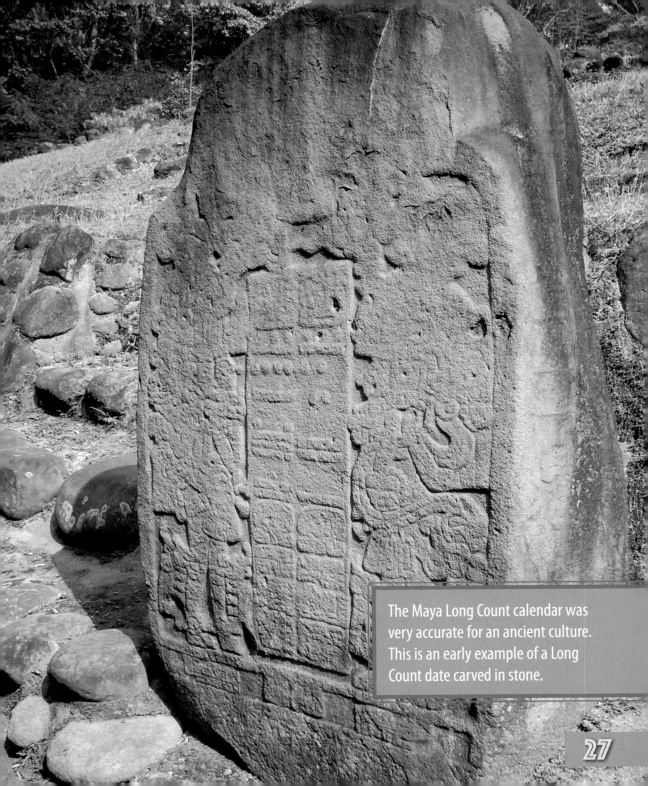

The Maya Long Count calendar was very accurate for an ancient culture. This is an early example of a Long Count date carved in stone.

FALL OF THE MAYA

As accurate as the Maya calendar was, it still couldn't predict the end of this great civilization. By AD 900, the Maya civilization was declining. Some believe the Maya lands suffered from droughts, or long periods of dry weather. Others suggest disagreements between the ruling class and commoners led to the Maya's downfall.

Eventually, the real end of the Maya civilization would come at the hands of European conquerors. In the early 1500s, the Spanish arrived in Mesoamerica. Spanish **conquistadors** like Francisco Hernández de Córdoba and Hernán Cortés came looking for gold and other riches. They also came looking for slaves.

Although the Maya were a strong people with fierce warriors, they were no match for the Spanish military and their superior technology. For many years they fought off the invaders, but by 1542, the Spanish had founded the city of Mérida within the region of the Maya. Those Maya who'd remained in their cities left to live in smaller villages.

Hernán Cortés was also responsible for the downfall of the mighty Aztec civilization. This relief carving shows a conquistador stepping on the heads of Maya.

HERNÁN CORTÉS

LEGACY OF THE MAYA

The Maya calendar still plays an important role in understanding the secrets of the Maya. With their advanced calendar, the Maya recorded events over long periods of time. Even today, this allows historians to study important events in Maya history.

The Maya are still regarded as one of the most advanced civilizations in the ancient world. They found a way to use the land and resources of Mesoamerica to build great city-states. Thanks to Maya technology, many of their great cities still stand as reminders of a once-great civilization. You can visit these cities to catch a glimpse of what it was like to live during the height of the Maya civilization.

Although the Maya civilization declined long ago, the **legacy** of their technological advances lives on. Historians and scientists alike are astonished at the inventions and techniques of this ancient civilization.

GLOSSARY

artifact (AAR-tih-fact): Something made by humans in the past that still exists.

canal (kuh-NAAL): A manmade waterway.

city-state (SIH-tee–STAYT): An independent city and the land around it.

commerce (KAH-murs): The large-scale buying and selling of goods and services.

conquistador (kahn-KEE-stuh-dohr): A Spanish conqueror or adventurer.

equinox (EE-kwih-nahx): A day when day and night are the same length. This happens twice a year.

iron ore (EYE-urn OHR): Rocks and minerals from which metallic iron can be taken.

legacy (LEH-guh-see): Something that is passed down from someone.

limestone (LYM-stohn): A stone often used to create buildings.

mortar (MOHR-tuhr): A soft building material that hardens when it dries.

observatory (uhb-ZUHR-vuh-toh-ree): A special building for studying space.

suspension bridge (suh-SPEN-shun BRIHJ): A bridge that's hung from two or more cables that are held up by towers.

technique (tehk-NEEK): A particular skill or ability that someone uses to perform a job.

INDEX

PRIMARY SOURCE LIST

Page 5: Temple I in Tikal. Built by the Maya people between 200 BC and AD 200. Stone. Located at the ancient site of Tikal in Petén Department, Guatemala.

Page 9 (jade ornament): Deity Face Pendant. Made by a Maya artisan between AD 600 and AD 700. Jade. Found in Guatemala or Mexico. Now kept at the Metropolitan Museum of Art, New York, New York.

Page 11: Temple of the Sun. Built by the Maya people around AD 690. Stone. Located at the ancient site of Palenque in Chiapas, Mexico.

Page 19: Fragment of the relief known as Tortuguero Monument 6. Created between AD 300 and AD 800. Stone. Found in Tabasco, Mexico. Now kept at the Metropolitan Museum of Art, New York, New York.

WEBSITES

Due to the changing nature of Internet links, PowerKids Press has developed an online list of websites related to the subject of this book. This site is updated regularly. Please use this link to access the list: www.powerkidslinks.com/soac/mayat